IMAGES
of America

GURNEE AND
WARREN TOWNSHIP

Warren township was created in December 1849, and in 1850 was named in honor of Maj. Gen. Joseph Warren, a Revolutionary War hero. Warren, a physician, was a leader of the Boston patriots who dispatched Paul Revere on his ride. General Warren was killed June 17, 1775, at the Battle of Bunker Hill, Charlestown, Massachusetts.

IMAGES
of America

GURNEE AND WARREN TOWNSHIP

Warren Township Historical Society

ARCADIA
PUBLISHING

Published by Arcadia Publishing
Charleston, South Carolina

Library of Congress Catalog Card Number: 2005936087

For all general information contact Arcadia Publishing at:
Telephone 843-853-2070
Fax 843-853-0044
E-mail sales@arcadiapublishing.com
For customer service and orders:
Toll-Free 1-888-313-2665

Visit us on the Internet at www.arcadiapublishing.com

*This book is dedicated to Warren's early settlers
and to charter members of the Warren Township
Historical Society, founded in 1976.*

CONTENTS

ACKNOWLEDGMENTS

As a historian, I am deeply indebted to those past historians who wrote the stories of Lake County, Gurnee and Warren Township. Edward Lawson's *History of Warren Township* (reprinted by Warren Township Historical Society) is a most valuable contribution and is the starting place for anyone attempting another history. Gilbert Clem's *Fifty Years of Change in Warren Township's Agriculture* details the township's rich farm heritage.

A valuable source of information for this book was our own historical society's archives, chronicling Gurnee and township events, which was started by founding member Lois Potter Balmes, who died in 1996. Her memorial funds were used to continue preservation of newspaper and other records. I owe a personal debt to Potter for insisting that I join the society in 1993 when I retired from teaching at Warren Township High School. Our work together was too brief.

People who contributed to this volume include historical society members Tom Mellen, Clarissa Mellen, Marge Miller, Ruth Brunke, Joyce Buehler, Don Haugh, Robert Haugh, Fran Courson, Marilyn See, Charlotte Renehan, Connie Klugiewicz, Joe Lodesky, Diana Dretske, and Al Westerman. Thanks to Westerman and Renehan for sharing their images. A special thanks goes to board member Michael Weiland for all of his efforts in scanning the images.

—Jill Martin, editor

INTRODUCTION

When Lake County adopted the township form of government in 1849, it was customary for settlers in each township to decide upon its name. Township 45 North, Range 11 East, a 16-square mile area divided by the Des Plaines River, became Warren Township in honor of Maj. Gen. Joseph Warren, killed at the Battle of Bunker Hill in 1775. Initially, the area had been known as O'Plaine, a variation of the river's name. O'Plaine was also the name of the local stagecoach stop and inn. During the term of Chicago mayor, "Long John" Wentworth, the area was known as Wentworth. By 1873, the Chicago, Milwaukee, and St. Paul Railroad crossed Warren Township. The local depot was named Gurnee Depot after Walter S. Gurnee, a member of the railroad board of directors and former mayor of Chicago. Soon the business district was also called Gurnee, and the name of the post office changed from Wentworth to Gurnee.

Today, Gurnee is the largest incorporated village within the boundaries of Warren Township, but it was by no means the township's only settlement. The area around the Abingdon Inn, near the corner of Milwaukee Road and Belvidere Road, became known as Abingdon. Gages Lake was settled early, as was Druce Lake. Warrenton, a school and post office, was also called Hartford and Wilson. An area near Route 120 was known as Saugatuck, and in the post-World War II era, areas such as Wildwood, Arbor Vista, and Orchard Valley evolved as distinct communities of western Warren. In 1958, Park City was formed from parts of Warren and Waukegan Townships.

A floating bridge, which crossed the Des Plaines River north of today's Grand Avenue bridge, brought early settlers to the oldest remaining building in Warren Township. In 1844, Jonathan Harvey and his wife, Wealthy, bought a log stage coach stop called the O'Plaine Tavern and subsequently built a larger inn, also the O'Plaine Tavern, across the road. Following Jonathan Harvey's death in 1845, Wealthy married Erastus Rudd in 1846, and the couple operated the stage coach stop while living nearby. The structure, referred to as Mother Rudd's, not only provided overnight accommodation to travelers, but also served as a post office and lively center of community activity. Local tradition has long held that the O'Plaine Tavern, or possibly its barn, was a stop on the Underground Railroad.

According to historian Edward Lawson, Warren's first school was located in the northwest section of the township. Other one-room schools serving the area's rural district soon appeared. By 1907, there were eight such schools totally or partially within the township. By the 1950s, most of the township's one-room schools outside the village consolidated to form Woodland School District 50. Two years of classes beyond the eighth grade were held at Woodman Hall, home of a social organization, until Warren Township High School on O'Plaine Road opened in the fall of 1917 with 64 students.

The first organized church in Gurnee met for 19 years at the Gurnee schoolhouse on Kilbourne Road before the construction in 1879 of a church building next to the school on land donated by Wealthy Rudd's son-in-law. In 1923, this building was moved to the site of the present Gurnee Community church and remodeled.

The Chicago, Milwaukee, and St. Paul Railroad connected Gurnee to Chicago and brought early tourists to the Grand Hotel, located next to the station. Later visitors came to lively festivals at the Vikings Club House—in a recreational park with rest home—established by the Order of Vikings on the same site as the hotel.

Post-World War II Gurnee became known for the Rustic Manor Restaurant that was destroyed by fire in 1987. Today, the same access to transportation that led to the success of Mother Rudd's Tavern has enabled Gurnee to develop entertainment and shopping facilities such as Great America and Gurnee Mills.

By sharing images from the Warren Township Historical Society's archives, the society hopes to inspire a richer appreciation of the past.

One

IN THE BEGINNING

The details of Warren Township's early settlement mirror those of much of Lake County with one notable exception. The first non-native settler in Warren Township, according to several historians, was a free African American man, Amos Bennett, who settled with his family along the Des Plaines River before 1835. His first neighbors were native Americans prior to their relocation to Wisconsin. The other settlers in Warren Township accepted Bennett as a neighbor, landowner, and voter, as documented by the appearance of his name in historical records. However, those records show that Bennett and his family left the area in the late 1850s. Most likely, the Dred Scott Decision of 1857, which left him vulnerable to capture and enslavement, forced his departure.

Other early settlers in Warren Township were, like Bennett, from New York or the New England states; such family names as Buell, Gage, Esty, Vose, and Blanchard appear in early records. Farmers came searching for arable land such as that bordering the Des Plaines River. The early roads crossing Warren Township made the area a good site for inns, and early post office sites such as Abingdon, Warrenton, and O'Plaine were located in inns or taverns.

Some early settlers were abolitionists. Two family stories tell of buildings used to protect escaped slaves as part of the Underground Railroad. Levi Stafford came to Warren Township in 1836 from Vermont. Stafford's granddaughter told of the comings and goings of African Americans on the family farm before the Civil War. About two miles away was the O'Plaine Tavern, a stage coach stop and inn built by Connecticut-born Jonathan Harvey and his wife, Wealthy. Following Harvey's death, Wealthy Buell Harvey Rudd and her second husband, Erastus Rudd, operated the inn. The O'Plaine Tavern and accompanying barn are reported to have been a stop on the Underground Railroad.

Newspapers of the Civil War era reported the Rudds' support of the war. Wealthy Rudd, known as a fine cook, held benefits for Union soldiers at the inn, and Erastus Rudd served as the area postmaster—at that time a political appointment—under Lincoln and subsequent Republican administrations. The people of Warren collectively echoed the Rudds' support of Lincoln. In fact, the community was awarded a large flag for its exceptional turnout in Chicago at Lincoln's second Chicago rally in 1864. The flag was displayed on a flagpole in front of Mother Rudd's until 1880.

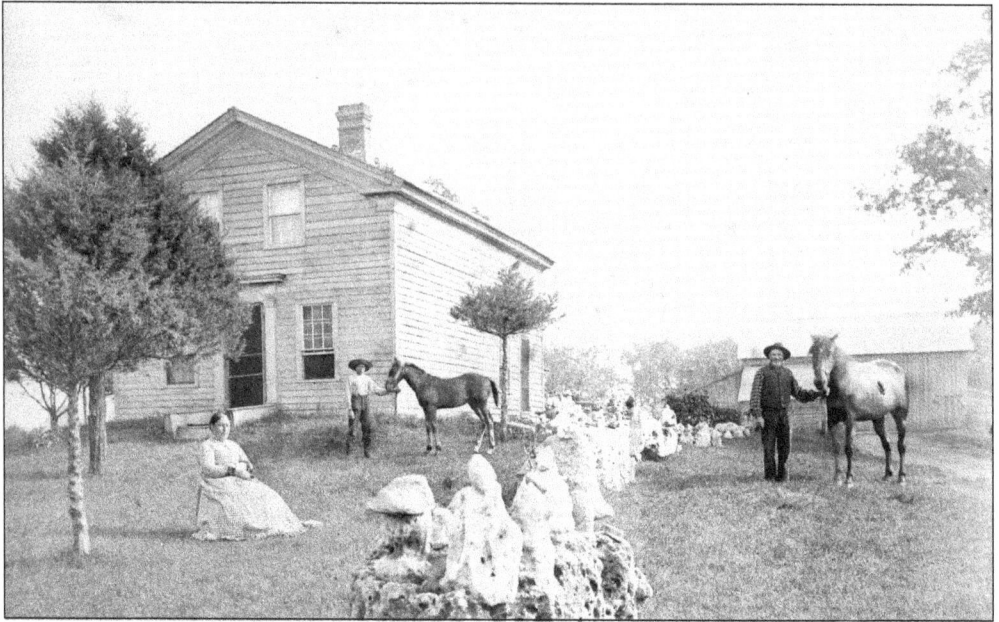

On the Stafford farm, a white frame house surrounded the original log cabin built by Levi Stafford, who is standing by the horse on the right. His granddaughter mentioned the barn as an Underground Railroad stop. The farm passed to the Faulkner family, and the Immanuel Baptist church now occupies the site.

In 1841, John Flood purchased 80 acres of land including that where the Viking School and Park District buildings now stand. He built this small house on that property.

An unidentified woman stands on the porch of the former O'Plaine Tavern next to the wooden frame of the "town pump." The well at the stagecoach stop was a reliable source of water for the early settlers and travelers. The building, in this c. 1910 image, was home to the family of Nancy Mutaw, daughter of Mother Rudd.

The barn behind the Mother Rudd Tavern was originally used to house horses for the stagecoaches. It was unroofed by wind in the 1970s and dismantled, leaving only the stone foundation. The barn possibly served as a shelter for escaped slaves on the Underground Railroad.

In the 20th century, the building once known as the O'Plaine Tavern became home to two generations of the McCann family. Thomas McCann and afterwards his son Hugh raised calves and shipped them to market from the Gurnee train depot.

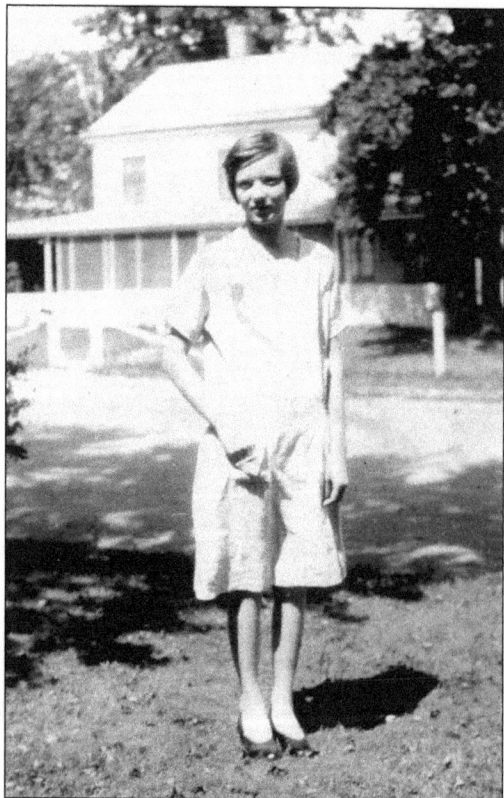

In 1927, Eileen Kimball posed in front of the McCann home. Older residents remember Mary McCann selling candy from a store inside the building's porch, probably added by the McCanns. The stump of the Civil War flag pole can be seen in the right background.

WARREN TOWNSHIP
HISTORICAL SOCIETY
COMMEMORATES
GURNEE'S OLDEST BUILDING
MOTHER RUDD'S TAVERN
C. 1840

THIS STRUCTURE WAS THE FOCAL POINT IN
THE EARLY DAYS OF THE WARREN TOWNSHIP
COMMUNITY. IT WAS IMPORTANT AS A STAGECOACH
STOP, INN, TAVERN, POST OFFICE, POLLING
PLACE, TOWN HALL, DANCE HALL, TOWN WELL
AND STATION ON UNDERGROUND RAILROAD.
NOW PRIVATELY OWNED.

The Rudd/McCann house was remodeled and given red siding by Dr. John and Patricia Kysar. On November 12, 1977, a historical marker was added by Warren Township Historical Society.

Waukegan school teacher Helen Gilmore and her husband Joseph lived in the Rudd/McCann house in the 1940s and 1950s. Former students still remember class picnics that she held on the property.

Horatio Buell built the two-story white farmhouse, known as the Chittenden house, of bricks made in a brick yard near Grand Avenue and Green Bay Road. Buell was the brother of Mother Rudd, as Wealthy Buell Harvey Rudd was known. Buell opened a small general store around 1840 on Milwaukee Avenue. Later, he became a merchant in Waukegan with a grocery store at Genesee and Washington Streets.

Ralph Chittenden's farm, on land first purchased by Horatio Buell, is now the site of Chittenden Park in Gurnee. Ralph Chittenden, who inherited the land from his father, John, a miller, lived there all his life.

A *c.* 1900 unidentified group visits Kuhn's Rock, a geologic feature rising above the landscape, which served as a reference point for escaped slaves traveling the Underground Railroad from northern Illinois to southern Wisconsin.

In 1978, members of the Warren Township Historical Society sat and stood upon Kuhn's rock, named for an early settler sympathetic to the cause of abolition. Identified here, from left to right, are (first row) Mary Welton, Tom Mellen, Wavie Swanson, Mary Stiehr, and Helen Leable; (second row) Georgianna Shaw, Clarissa Mellen, and Alice Johnson; (third row) Beverly Dole, Beverly Shaw, Herman Stier, Kenneth Leable, Art Welton, and Elbert Elsbury.

15

Wealthy Buell Harvey Rudd was buried beneath this stone in Warren Cemetery. Also known as Mother Rudd, she was born in Connecticut in 1793 and died in 1880. She was married two times, outliving both husbands. After the death of her first husband, Jonathan Harvey, she married widower Erastus Rudd. Together they operated the O'Plaine Tavern, better known as Mother Rudd's place.

Elizabeth Wells Bidwell, shown in later life, was one of the first two women elected to the Gurnee school board in the 1870s, long before women could vote in national elections. She and her farmer husband Thomas were active in the community and were members of the Episcopal Church. Both were buried in Union Cemetery.

Two

FARMS AND ESTATES

The early farmers who purchased land in Warren Township found the soil well adapted to raising spring wheat. Their crops were first harvested by hand by cradling the grain. By 1849, horse-pulled reapers reduced the time and effort of harvesting. Other developments in farm machinery improved grain output. Agriculture teacher Gilbert Clem's history of the township's farming recorded that Warren Township had some of the most fertile land in Lake County.

After the Civil War, farmers turned to improved varieties of poultry, pigs, and dairy cattle. In 1917, the township's farmers raised 10 varieties of poultry. By 1931, over 100 farmers had dairy herds and supplied a local dairy plant and customers in Waukegan, as well as shipping milk to Chicago by train. As Warren's agriculture changed to livestock farming, the area became known for dairy production.

The township was also home to several large estates with local managers; the owners lived in Chicago and suburbs such as Lake Forest. Estates included the Bartholomay family's Marellbar estate, which raised champion Oxford sheep, the Thomas Wilson estate, Edellyn Farms, known for prize shorthorn cattle, and the Richard W. Sears estate on Gages Lake, home to the founder of Sears, Roebuck, and Company.

Housing and business developments have overtaken most of these farming areas, leaving very little agriculture in the township.

The Potter family farmhouse, near Washington and Milwaukee Road, is pictured around 1960 with the Des Plaines River in the background. When Edwin Potter returned to Lake County after serving with the 96th Illinois Infantry during the Civil War, he purchased this farm.

Edwin Potter's son Alonzo "Lonnie" Potter inherited the farm and lived there with his wife Cynthia (Harris) Potter and family. Lonnie is haying on his land, around 1900.

Seen behind the Potter's abandoned silo is the American Eagle wooden roller coaster ride at Great America Theme Park. Development marked the decline of farming in the township.

The Shaw barn and farmhouse, home of Emery Shaw and wife Sarah (Adams) Shaw, were on Blanchard and Yorkhouse Roads. The family moved to Warren Township in 1926 and raised chickens, ducks, pigs, and cows.

Several generations of the Lamb family lived on both sides of Edic Road (now Hunt Club Road) at Grand Avenue. Joseph Lamb acquired the land in 1839 and built a saw mill before a trip to the California gold fields. The Carl and Bess Lamb house is pictured here.

A self-portrait by Nahan "Ney" Lamb who was a grandson of Joseph. Ney was raised at Lamb's Corners and replaced the original home with a new one. Ney Lamb, a man of many talents, was known as a professional photographer, musician, painter, storyteller, and rug-hooker.

A threshing crew posed at the Nahum Lamb farm in 1896. Nahum Lamb, son of Joseph Lamb, fought with the 96th Illinois in the Civil War. After his return, he farmed and ran a feed mill at Lamb's Corners together with family members.

The McClure farmhouse was on Grand Avenue, across from the Viking property. The McClure family farm became part of the business district of Gurnee. McClure's Garage is presently on the property.

A seed salesman stood with Charles Dooley, a founding member of the historical society, before a field of corn in Warren Township during the 1960s. At that time it took a month to harvest a field with a one-row chopper. (Courtesy of the Lodesky family.)

22

Farming was a family business. The women, preparing dinner for the hands, were called from their kitchen to pose with the men and horses in this scene at haying time.

Elbert Elsbury, noted for his Holstein dairy herd, was very active in the farming community. The Elsbury farm was located off Highway 132. Elbert Elsbury began farming in 1912 after the death of his father on the *Titanic*. His last crop was planted in 1975 before his farm sale in March 1976 ended an era.

In 1913, this cement block house on Dilley's Road was built on the Chandler farm for a farmhand. Three Chandler brothers came to Warren Township from Pennsylvania in 1843 in order to farm. The child seated on the rug is a member of the Faulkner family who lived in the house in 1922, the date of this photograph. (Courtesy of Tom Mellen.)

In 1961, the cement block house on Dilley's Road is seen in a changed landscape. The view was altered when the land was no longer used for farming. (Courtesy of Tom Mellen.)

Here is a view of the C. A. Faulkner farm on Dilley's Road, earlier owned by the Stafford family. In addition to their dairy herd, the Faulkner brothers raised Chester White hogs.

Farms passed from family to family. In 1879, the Metcalf family owned Maple Town Farm. Other family names associated with this house and property are Snyder and Martin. The house later became a restaurant and doctor's office, and is now a commercial property on Grand Avenue near Dilley's Road.

The land on which the Warren-Newport Library was built in 1973 has had a long farm history. The George McCullough house is pictured, but the land was also farmed by the Potter and Dunham families.

The Whitmore farm was on Edic (Hunt Club) Road near Grange Hall Road, now called Washington Street. Alfred D. Whitmore originally purchased 40 acres in 1852. Whitmore was active in building a school, known as Grange Hall School, on the land.

Beverly Dole used the old Grange Hall as a storage building on his Washington Street farm. Organized in 1867, the Grange was a fraternal and social organization for farmers. Their hall was a local gathering place.

The farm buildings on the northwest corner of Stearns School Road and Hunt Club Road were part of the C. L. Vose farm around 1900.

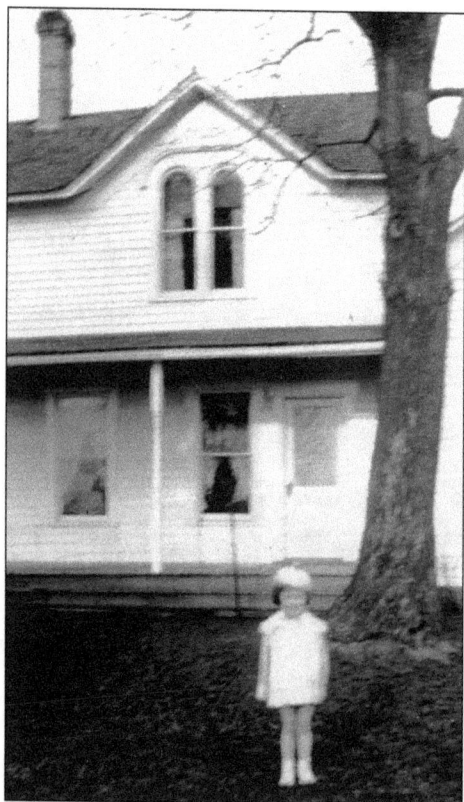

A young member of the Lamb family posed in front of a farmhouse at Lamb's Corners, as the corner of Hunt Club and Grand Avenue was once known.

William Duncan, the manager of Willam Bartholomay's Marellbar Farm, showed the farm's champion Oxford sheep.

Marellbar Farm estate off River Road featured extensive stone buildings. Bartholomay was a nationally known breeder of Oxford sheep.

William Bartholomay's daughter Margaret is seen visiting with one of the farm's Oxford sheep in 1934.

Oxford sheep posed before the entrance to Marellbar Farm near River Road in Warren Township around 1930. The farm is still privately owned.

Thomas Wilson, owner of Wilson Meat Packing Company, purchased 2,000 acres in Warren and Libertyville Townships for Edellyn Farms. He spent much time at this home located near what is now Fountain Square. The names of the area's school and train depot were changed from Warrenton to Wilson. (Courtesy of Robert Haugh.)

The annual sale of prize shorthorn cattle on Thomas Wilson's estate, such as this one around 1945, attracted buyers from across the nation. All the visitors were treated to a picnic lunch served at Edelynn Farms. (Courtesy of Robert Haugh.)

In this winter scene at the Richard W. Sears estate, children waited for a sled ride. The 20-room mansion was owned first by Sears, then later by Tom Rule. The house was struck by lightning in 1969 and partially destroyed. (Courtesy of Grayslake Historical Society.)

A horse drawn cart served as transportation on the Sears estate. In this scene, from left to right, are Jane Drummond Maebak, Willard Mogg, Ruth Drummond Mogg, and Ricky Sears. (Courtesy of Grayslake Historical Society.)

Tom a his Ford car 1920

The Sears estate manager's Ford was parked in front of a horse barn built on the estate in 1920 by the Rich brothers and Will Neal. (Courtesy of Grayslake Historical Society.)

Tom Mogg, the Sears estate manager, and his wife Emma lived in this Sears pre-cut home built for them around 1919. Plans, lumber, and supplies for these homes were purchased from the Sears catalog.

The east side of Warren Township was home to the area's only pony farm, owned by Richard and Ellen Jenkins. One of their prize-winning ponies, Mr. Bay Boy, is shown winning a harness race at Hudsonville, Michigan, in 1970.

Three

HOMES

From the village's beginning, a combination of homes and businesses populated the street now called Old Grand Avenue and the neighboring Delany and Depot Roads. Many of the earliest houses are lost, but several houses have survived for over 100 years. Only images remain of others as newer homes and businesses have supplanted them on a street that still combines homes and businesses.

Two grand buildings that remain are the Bidwell and Sponenburg homes. The home built by the Bidwell sisters, Josie and Delia, is now a funeral home. Sherman Sponenburg's house still remains a family home. The rooming house for railroad workers stands next to the Chicago, Milwaukee, and St. Paul Railroad tracks. Merchants and professional men built more modest homes on the street in order to live near their work. Park Smith lived across the street from his hardware store and Frank McGarva, near his blacksmith shop. Each individual's home had a personality, built to its owner's taste.

The family homes of farmers Norman Brown and Thomas McClure were on Grand Avenue with their land stretching out beyond the houses. The old homes that remain give a glimpse of the street as it once was.

The Washburn house on Old Grand Avenue, east of the railroad, was originally built as a rooming house for railroad workers and has been home to several generations of the Washburn family.

Willis Appleyard, station master of the Gurnee Railroad Depot, lived in this home on Old Grand Avenue, close to his work.

The Milner/Holst house, on the north side of Old Grand Avenue, was originally a summer home. Fay Milner, a Chicago school teacher, used the house in the summer. Then the Holst family lived there. The original property was given by Mother Rudd to her daughter Martha and son-in-law Henry Cone.

A street scene from a postcard shows houses on Old Grand Avenue, looking east. Houses visible from left to right belonged to Will McCullough, Margaret Thorn, and Pastor Amstutz.

The Babcock, Chase, and Jack McClure families occupied this home on Old Grand Avenue at Delaney Road. The house was believed to have been a hotel before being moved to the present site.

A horse is practicing with a trainer in front of an early 20th century Gurnee hotel building.

Behind the Peter Stewart house on Old Grand Avenue, a paint crew on scaffolding is shown painting the top level.

A well-digging crew worked at the Peter Stewart house on Old Grand Avenue, installing a well behind the home.

Shown here is the distinctive Wakefield/Cunningham home on Old Grand Avenue as it appeared in the early 20th century.

Laura and Leander W. Wakefield lived in the Old Grand Avenue home in 1900, following their 1899 marriage.

The Shepard home on the corner of Old Grand Avenue and Delaney Road was another house occupied by several generations of a family.

Ben F. Shepard worked on the lawn as his wife watched from the porch of their home in Gurnee. Shepard served as a sergeant in the 96th Illinois Infantry during the Civil War.

The Haines house, pictured on Old Grand Avenue, is now the site of LaCasa, a service organization.

Members of the Haines family gathered in front of their home. Howell Haines was a blacksmith who played the violin. Haines's daughters Maime, Estella, and Ethel lived in the house for most of their long lives.

42

The Henry Marsh family home was on Delaney Road. A grandfather of the Marsh family settled in Warren Township in 1836.

The Dan Doyle house was moved from Kilbourne Road and Old Grand Avenue to McClure Road, near Gowe Park and the Des Plaines River. Later additions are seen in this photograph taken after the move.

The Bidwell/Stedman house was on Old Grand Avenue. The Bidwell sisters, Josie and Adela, were the daughters of Thomas and Elizabeth Wells Bidwell, and they were a family active in community affairs.

Midge Stedman and a friend pose in an undated image. The Stedman family lived in the Bidwell house, now used as the Gurnee Funeral Home.

Seen here is the Smith/Tobin house on Old Grand Avenue, around 1912. Park Smith owned a hardware store across from his home. Joseph and Sally Tobin purchased the house in 1976 from Smith's widow. (Courtesy of Joe Tobin.)

The Nehemiah Chubb house on Depot Road was built by Chubb, a native of England. Chubb and his wife Pollyana both worked for the Bidwell sisters, helping to care for their large home and yard.

Old Grand Avenue is on the left of the postcard pictured. The three houses on the right belonged to Lee Miller, Sherman Sponenburg, and Park Smith.

The Marion and Betsy Schryver house is on O'Plaine Road across from the high school. A small brick building in the rear was a mortuary used by Schryver in his business as an undertaker.

This home off Old Grand Avenue was owned by the McCormick family, then Marion Decker, and then Dr. Ed and Carol May.

The Sponenburg house is on Old Grand Avenue. After Hiram Sponenburg patented his invention for the "Railway-Rail Stay," a device to keep rails secure, he built this home around 1910.

Norman Brown built a home on the corner of Depot Road and Old Grand Avenue. His adjoining farm became a sub-division known as Brown Circle, and the site of his home is now an apartment building.

John McGarva built his house next to his blacksmith shop. The McGarva house on Old Grand Avenue became the Werenski home and barber shop before being razed.

Boys are seen playing on Old Grand Avenue near the road leading to the Viking Home. Ed Gillings is in the cart, pulled by a pony ridden by his brother Gordon Gillings. LaVerne Dixon rides in the middle, and on the right is Bill Thomas.

The McClure/Dixon house was on the corner of Old Grand Avenue and O'Plaine Road, on a site currently being developed as a bank. Dr. L. J. McClure, a veterinarian, lived there before the Ray Dixon family.

This two-story brick house was built in 1877 by Adolphus Wustenfeld, then sold to Thomas McClure. It was home to George Dalziel and his wife, later to Bill Hook, and then to John Conelly.

Four

CHURCHES
AND CEMETERIES

According to historian Edward Lawson, the first organized church in Gurnee was established in 1856–1857 and called the Church of Christ. Members worshipped in the school on Kilbourne Road until a church was built next to the school in 1878. In 1885, an organ was purchased to accompany the church's choir.

In 1923, the church building was physically moved several blocks to the site now occupied by the present, recently remodeled Gurnee Community Church. The church's history represents a continuity in worship from the 19th through the 21st centuries.

Other denominations began worship services in the area of Gages Lake and at Stafford's Corners, but histories of those have not survived. The Methodist church at Stafford's Corners, Stearns School Road and Dilley's Road, was moved to the corner of Green Bay and Yorkhouse Roads.

Warren Township is the site of the St. Sava Serbian Orthodox Church, Monastery, and Seminary, established in 1927 on Milwaukee Avenue. In the last half of the 20th century many places of worship appeared in Gurnee and Warren Township.

Warren Cemetery was established in 1846 by a group of early settlers who purchased a three-acre parcel near the center of the Township from William Boswell for $24. In 1847, a fence was erected around part of the newly named Warren Cemetery. In 1873, a group of ladies formed the Warren Cemetery Association in order to operate the cemetery and raise money for improvements. The first year they raised $600. In 1891, the association was incorporated, and another acre of land purchased and fenced.

In 1895, fund-raising began for a soldier's monument in the cemetery, and in 1902, the monument was dedicated. A chapel was built in 1917 after further fund-raising efforts. The cemetery now covers nearly 30 acres. Until the 1990s, the Warren Cemetery Association operated the cemetery.

The Gurnee Church was moved in 1923 from the Kilbourne Road site to Old Grand Avenue where it was remodeled and enlarged. The rear addition is seen to the left of this view taken shortly after the move.

The Gurnee Christian Church was built in 1878 on Kilbourne Road. This view of the church is dated 1893. Notice the balloon from the Chicago Columbian Exposition seen above the trees. The Gurnee Grade School can be seen to the right of the church.

As part of the remodeling of the Gurnee church, stained glass windows were inserted in the front of the church and on each side of the entrance, as seen in this view taken after the move to Old Grand Avenue.

St. Sava Serbian Church and Monastery, built in 1927, is located on Milwaukee Avenue, in the southern part of the township. The church building contains the tomb of Peter II, king of the former nation of Yugoslavia. He is the only European monarch buried on American soil.

A monument on the grounds of St. Sava Serbian Church and Monastery honors the Yugoslavian patriot Draza Mihailevich (1907–1945).

Women of the Warren Cemetery Association gathered at an outing to the Lake County jail in Waukegan with the jailer's wife as hostess. Identified here are Susie Van Alstine, Cora Denman, Miss Dunlap, Cynthia Miller, Cora L. McCullough, Cornelia Wilbur, Eliza Beck, Ellen Lamb, Mary Lamb, Florence Brandstetter, Mary Wilbur, Lucy Estes, Elizabeth Wooley, Jane Griffin, Ada Whitmore, Alma Rose, Jane McGuire, Clara Hook, Nellie Cashmore, Minetta Bonner, and Kitty Clow.

The Soldiers Monument in Warren Cemetery was dedicated "In Honor of the Soldiers of Lake Co., Ill." on June 8, 1902. Estella "Stella" Vose, age 8, was chosen to pull the cord at the unveiling of the monument. Stella Vose Faulkner, born May 27, 1894, died September 23, 2002, at age 108.

The stone chapel at the Warren Cemetery was dedicated in the fall of 1917. The Warren Cemetery Association donated one of the large stained glass windows at the front of the chapel, other windows were donated by individuals in memory of their loved ones.

The boys' Sunday School class meets at the Gurnee church around 1920. Seen here, from left to right, are (first row) Mahlon Washburn, William Dixon, Robert Stedman, Donald Mills, and Elmer Russell; (second row) George Murrie, William Flood, Allan Flood, Melvin Hook, and Clyde Wutzke; (third row) LaVerne Dixon, Everett McClure, Edward Gillings, Mr. Hanley, Dean Ray, and Howard Smith.

Five

SCHOOLS

The eight rural school houses in Warren Township included Gages Lake School, Druce Lake School, Vose School, Grange Hall School, Stafford School, Saugatuck School, Stearns School, and Warrenton, later called Wilson School. The present Gurnee Grade School is on the site of the town's first school. Some students from Warren Township also attended Town Line, Spaulding, Millburn, and Dodge.

Schools were first given district numbers but were soon called by names reflecting the donor of the land, as in Vose and Stafford; the area in Warren Township, as in Saugetuck or Warrenton; or the road's name, such as Grange Hall. Of course, the name of Stearns School Road has outlived the school. Of these early schools, only two buildings remain—one as a private home and the other as a florist shop.

In 1948, a referendum offered residents in the township's rural school districts the option to combine into a single district. The resultant District 50 Woodland School opened in 1953. This action 50 years ago established the state's sixth largest grade school district with an enrollment of more than 7,000 in 2005.

The Gurnee school district consolidated with Town Line School and Wadsworth School and absorbed part of Spaulding, using the North Spaulding School since 1976. Viking Middle School was built in 1970 on the grounds of the Independent Order of Valhalla property, and Milton Davis became superintendent.

Warren Township High School opened in 1917, only to be closed briefly by an influenza epidemic. To accommodate the rural nature of the area, the school began with an agriculture department, believed to be the first in the state. In 1920, a model-farm shop was constructed north of the high school; the agriculture classes continued until 1961. A 1964 addition altered the front view of the high school. After a disastrous fire in December 1984 destroyed much of the building, a new building opened in 1987, on the site of the original school.

The early brick building housing the Gages Lake School, shown in this *c.* 1900 photograph, was located on Highway 45, south of Gages Lake Road.

The two-room brick Gages Lake School was built around 1900, and used until 1954, when the district was consolidated with Woodland School District. The Gages Lake School building was sold in 1958 and is a florist shop today.

Nathaniel Vose donated land for a log school which opened in 1843, located in Section 17. The frame Vose School opened in 1853 on Grand Avenue. After consolidation with Stearns School, the early school, shown here, was sold to R. E. Hook and moved to be used for a pig barn.

Students in the Vose School photograph, from left to right, are Horace Vose, Charles Hook, Lula Vose, Emma Brexen, teacher Miss Odett, John Brewer, Gertrude Brewer, and George Clark. Vose School consolidated with Stearns School in 1908.

Early settlers John and Alvira Shepard Stearns donated land for Stearns School where Alvira taught. A building erected in 1854 was replaced by a brick school built in 1924 for nearly $9,000. The old frame school was sold, moved, and converted into a home.

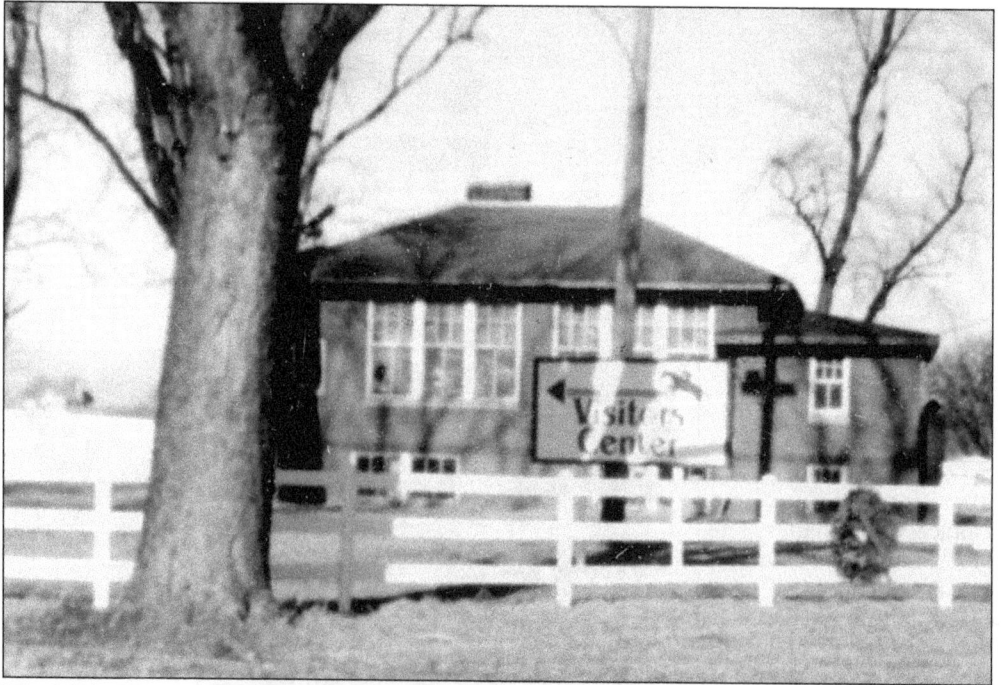

The brick Stearns School building and site was sold in 1954 to Douglas Stuart who used it as a farm building and visitors center for Hunt Club Estates before its removal.

In 1896, Grange Hall School included teacher Ollie Knox holding Myrtle Wilbur and students Jessie Schryver, Jennie Schryver, Grover Studer, Dick Clapham, John Clapham, Rudy Miltmore, Blane H. Miltmore, Pearl Wilbur, Edith Beck, Jessie Beck, Charles Clapham, Lavilla Wilbur, L. Wilbur, G. D. Funkun, George DeForest, Amy Clapham, Doris Dewey, and Emma Studer.

In 1854, a frame building, later called Grange Hall School, was constructed on Whitmore property at the corner of the present Hunt Club Road and Washington Street. Some students group at the door with the teacher, others play at the well pump.

The later brick Grange Hall School was sold in 1954 as part of the consolidation forming Woodland School District. The building served as a club meeting hall for the 40 and 8, a local veterans group, until it was razed for commercial use.

In the interior of the one-room Grange Hall School, students pose with percussion instruments in June 1956.

Saugatuck School served students from Warren as well as Libertyville addresses. The school was sold in 1954 and used as a home until it was razed in order to widen Milwaukee Avenue, near Belvidere Road.

SOUVENIR

SAUGATUCK SCHOOL
DISTRICT NUMBER 54
WARREN, Lake County, ILLINOIS

SEPTEMBER 9, 1901—JUNE 24, 1902

Presented By

Emma E. Studer, *Teacher*

SCHOOL BOARD

A. Lodeski   L. A. Russell
E. E. Marsh   M. W. Marvin, Co. Sup't

PUPILS

George Campbell	Celia Lodeski
Charlie Hook	Laura McCann
William Foudrey	Florence Lodeski
Gomer Hopkins	Pearl Russell
Walter Russell	Agnes Campbell
James Callahan	Mae Brogden
Harry Brogden	Tillie Wallenter
John Beitzel	Cora Hook
Dennis Cawley	Pearl McCann
John Wallenter	Margaret Gallagher
Willie Chandler	Mary Lodeski
John Callahan	Sarah McCann
Willie Stoerp	Verna Russell
Henry Suhling	Myrtle Strong
Jake Beitzel	Hazel Strong
Willie Kneasley	Amber Colby
George Hagner	Minnie Stoerp
Hugh McCann	Hattie Russell
Paul Stoerp	Loretta Thomas
George Kneasley	Mabel Chandler
Frank Stoerp	Ethel O'Neil
Fred Amann	Willie Beitzel
George Callahan	Frank McCann
Joe Lodeski	Leonard Strong
Harry Beitzel	Hattie Amann
Edith Russell	Emma Kneasley
Nellie Hook	Rose Kneasley
	Dorothy Marsh

MEYRUGTOR CO., DANSVILLE, N. Y.

Teacher Emma Studer, of Saugatuck School, gave graduating students a souvenir bookmark at the close of school. Fifty-five students were taught by Emma Studer during the 1902 school year. Only 15 students attended the school in 1940.

The third log school built in the township was called Crocker School. The school was relocated to Dilley's Road, on Levi Stafford's property, and renamed Stafford School. The brick school shown here remains as a private home.

Seen here is a Stafford School class around 1940. The brick school building, constructed in 1928, was sold at auction in 1954 for use as a private residence.

Warrenton School was organized in 1874 by Daniel McCarthy and Philip Sheridan. The school opened with 73 students aged 6 to 22. John Kelly, a Civil War veteran, was the first teacher. In 1918, the original frame school was replaced by a brick one. Evidently when the train station was renamed Wilson, the school name changed as well. The school was surrounded on three sides by the Thomas Wilson property, Edllyn Farms estate.

The brick Wilson School, pictured in 1918, was sold in 1954 and used as a private residence until razed for highway widening of Belvidere Road, Route 120.

Seen here are students grouped outside Wilson School, around 1940, with teacher Katherine Lux in the back row.

Druce Lake School was located on the east side of Highway 45 and Rollins Road. The school was sold in 1958 for commercial use. A victim of highway widening, the building was razed in 2005.

Early in the area's history, the school serving the Gurnee area was moved to Kilbourne Road, the site of the present Gurnee Grade School, as shown in 1900. There have been at least four school buildings and additions on the Kilbourne Road site.

Gurnee students, including the high school students standing on the stairs, are gathered in front of the three-room school around 1900. The Woodman Hall was also used as a school before the high school was built.

These students at Gurnee Grade School in 1923 were taught by Helen Mainwaring and Arthur Howard.

The 1893 Gurnee Grade School at the left remained after the addition was built in 1964.

A *c.* 1930 interior view of the Gurnee Grade School classroom shows students at desks.

An exterior view of Gurnee Grade School in 1964 shows a new addition to the left of where the 1893 school once was.

This is the groundbreaking ceremony in 1965 for Viking Junior High School with, from left to right, Ollie Moller, Pastor Julius Koch, Wallace Ames, John Shelinger, John Cunningham, William Loblaw, Rayner Swanson, and Pastor John Devine.

An exterior view shows Viking School in 1987 before it was razed for a new middle school.

The Woodland School building on Gages Lake Road demonstrates the size of the school that combined seven rural schools into one district. (Courtesy of Cindy Mellen.)

Marguerite Messersmith was a long time teacher in Warren schools. She taught first grade at Woodland for 26 years. Every year she gave each student a personalized photo album.

Spaulding School North on Gurnee's east side is seen in a 1959 view. Spaulding South was closed and Spaulding North consolidated with Gurnee schools.

Warren Township's high school opened in 1917 after completion of a one-story brick building on today's O'Plaine Road. The two doors on the building's front provided separate entrances for boys and girls.

The first graduation at the high school in 1921 was marked by a "yearbook," a booklet showing the school's modern classrooms. In this view young ladies in the commercial room are training to become secretaries. (Courtesy of Warren Township High School.)

The high school's window-filled woodworking room offered boys the opportunity to make practical or whimsical objects, such as the model barn on the table. (Courtesy of Warren Township High School.)

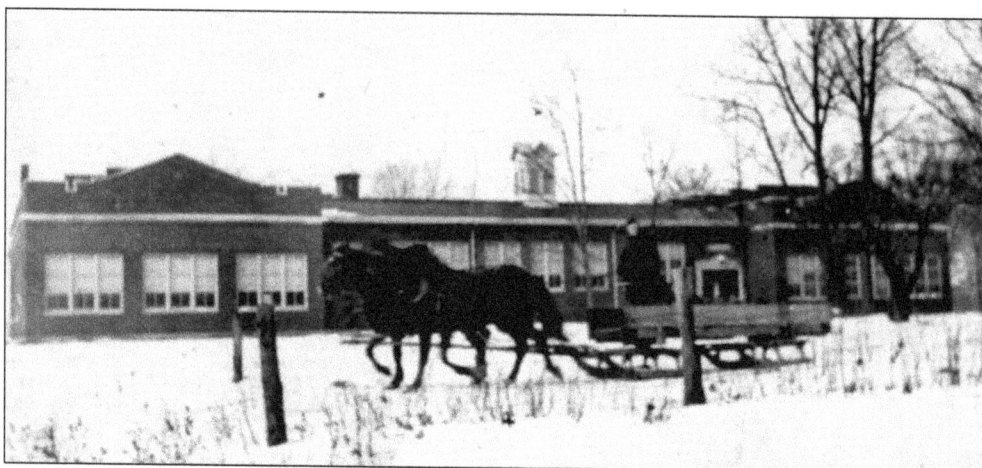

Warren High School in 1920 was the destination for a winter sleigh ride. Here a wagon is transformed into a two-horse sleigh in a scene captured on a postcard. That year snowstorms closed the school for three days in January.

In 1926 a second story, the first of many expansions, was added to the high school, as the school's population outgrew the space provided in the original one-story building.

The Warren High School basketball team is gathered here around 1930. The players are, from left to right, (first row) Bill Snyder, Ralph Potter, Bill Hook, Rusty Cannon, Bob Dixon, and Edward Zimmerman; (second row) Coach Robert Kelton, Ken Zimmerman, Fran Ptasenski, Virgil Lewin, Ray Rawling, and Ernie Turnpaugh.

Gurnee's fire trucks are parked beside the 1964 addition to the high school.

Agriculture teacher Gilbert "Gib" Clem paused after leaving the agriculture classes building in 1955. Warren High School offered agriculture classes for 42 years. For 30 years, Gib Clem taught farming practices to students, including some girls. He retired in 1971 after 40 years at Warren. (Courtesy of Warren Township High School.)

Students from Warren's junior class presented the play *Little Women* on the school's stage in December 1936. (Courtesy of Warren Township High School.)

Six

BUSINESSES AND ORGANIZATIONS

After the first "floating bridge" was built across the Des Plaines River, possibly by Erastus Rudd, commerce spread to both sides of the river and intertwined with homes. Records show that in 1861, two blacksmiths and a general merchandise store, as well as several inns, were established in the village. By 1900, business in the village had expanded to include two grocers, three blacksmiths, a woman photographer, a milliner, a creamery, two hotels, and an egg dealer as well as teachers, carpenters, and others. Of the villagers listed in the 1900 census of Warren Township, two-thirds were farmers. However, the growth of resorts was reflected in a rise in non-farm occupations such as hotel or summer resort managers.

Farmers joined the Society of Grangers, a fraternal and social organization for farmers. In 1876, members built a two-story Grange hall at the intersection of Washington and Hunt Club Roads (formerly Grange Hall and Edic Roads). Farmers, as well as others, joined the Modern Woodmen of America, a social and insurance organization with a building in Gurnee.

Historian Edward Lawson described a "cheese factory," located across from Mother Rudd's Tavern, that operated as a cooperative business using milk from township farms. There were a number of cider mills in the township. The Bowman Dairy Company on Depot Road purchased milk from local dairymen. When George and Thomas McClure bought the former Barney Hicks farm, they developed land near the Des Plaines River as a source of gravel for area roads. This land later became the village's swimming area, popularly called the "Pit."

Following World War II the Trybom family opened the Rustic Manor Restaurant on the corner of Route 132 and Kilbourne Road, widely known as much for its décor as for its food. The Rustic Manor was so famous in the Chicago and Milwaukee area that tour buses stopped there before a fire destroyed the building in 1985.

A portion of this view of the Bracher and Dixon General Store appears on this book's cover. The two buildings in this charming image still exist in altered form on the north side of Old Grand Avenue.

Citizens posing in front of the Bracher and Dixon store and post office, known as "Headquarters," are identified from left to right as Hughie Hughes, George Dalziel, unknown, Ernie Worth, James Campbell, Will Washburn, Fred Behrens, Leslie McClure, R. W. McClure, Frank Shepard, Roy Bracher, Leo Hook, Wesley Strang, Van Ness Young, and William Albright. Norman Brown's house appears on the left side.

In the 1950s, Old Grand Avenue was home to a number of stores on the north side of the road, east of the railroad. The buildings were, from the left, Gurnee Heating and Sheet Metal, a house once occupied by Leo Fenlon, Gungler's Drugs, and two others.

Depke's Garage and Jeep dealership was flooded in 1960. Justus Depke began the business in 1929 as a garage and Standard Gasoline station. The renovated building is still a commercial site.

The Dunning grocery store, seen here around 1900, was on the west side of the Viking property. Later the house was owned by Fred Wirth, then moved to the south side of Old Grand Avenue, and used by B. K. Mills as a tin shop.

In the 1920s, McClure's Garage, on the left, sold and repaired Ford automobiles. The apartment on the second floor was home to switchboard operator Loretta Ray and her son. The Warren Mutual Telephone Company switchboard was located there.

The Gurnee butcher Gabriel Odette, who served customers in Gurnee and Waukegan, posed for photographer Ney Lamb.

The home of the Bidwell sisters and the Stedman family became the site of the Gurnee Funeral Home in the 1970s.

Here is the Park Smith Hardware store as it appeared around 1950. The building was moved from Depot Road to Old Grand Avenue around 1925.

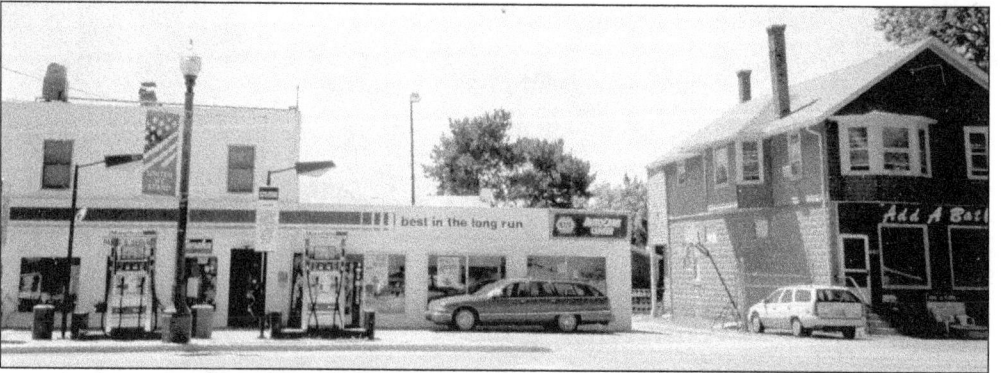

McClure's Garage, which opened in 1910 and is still in operation with a fourth generation, is seen in a recent view. The building on the right was once occupied by the Keel Grocery.

An interior view of the McClure Garage taken in the 1930s shows, from left to right, employees Bill Dalziel, Doug McCaughey, Joe Dada, and an African-American man identified as an employee of the McCaughey family.

Worth's Garage was on the corner of Highway 21 and Grand Avenue. Originally a Standard station, the garage was owned by Bob Worth, who lived in the house on the right.

The Bowman Dairy Company and Bottling Plant was located on Depot Road near Highway 41, with a siding close to railroad tracks. Later the building was used as a pickle factory and a paint factory.

Employees who gathered outside the Bowman Dairy Company building include, fifth from left to right, Lynn Vincent, Fred Stedman, George Winters, Clarence Crawford, Jimmy Chubb, an unidentified workman, and Harvey Nolan.

A fire destroyed Bennett's Cider Mill on Old Grand Avenue on March 23, 1910. This image taken just after the fire offered a view of the buildings, from left to right, Hicks Barn and outbuildings; a tin shop, probably belonging to B. K. Mills; a store with a façade; the Grey home; and the Austin home, just visible on the right.

This two-story frame building, once located near the present fire department, housed the hall of the Modern Woodmen of America, an insurance and benevolent organization. The building functioned as a social center for the first half of the 20th century and briefly housed high school students.

The Woodmen's Hall was the site of the annual Homecoming picnic. Participants pose in this early scene.

The Modern Woodmen of America included, as auxiliary organizations, the Royal Neighbors of America and the Benevolent Maidens. This group of c. 1900 Maidens included from left to right (first row) Eva Wilbur, Flossie Johnson, Pearl Wilbur, Dora Gullidge, Lavenia Sylvester, and Cynthia Potter; (second row) Minetta Denman, Ruby Knox, and Edith Van Alstin; (third row) Eva Esty, Mary Eichinger, Lula Vose, and Stella Vose.

In a celebration of Armistice Day, Frank Stedman and J. R. Bracher, in a woman's costume, rode in a cart pulled by a decorated donkey.

Following World War II, the Trybom family opened the Rustic Manor Restaurant, a unique western-styled eatery across from the Mother Rudd house.

The interior of the Rustic Manor Restaurant featured a waterfall as well as numerous taxidermist's examples like the bear.

At Christmas time, the Rustic Manor Restaurant was decorated with an antique sleigh pulled by a stuffed deer. The bar area seating included a bench built around a tree that later died.

Seven

FIRE, POLICE, MAIL, AND GOVERNMENT

Even small villages need police and fire protection. In the early years, a volunteer bucket brigade tried to save buildings, and a constable represented law enforcement. After 1951, when a police tax was passed, Gurnee's fire and police departments shared a single building on Old Grand Avenue, near the present fire department. There was one policeman, who replaced the local constable, and a volunteer fire department summoned by the telephone operator Loretta Ray. The fire truck was kept behind McClure's Garage.

During the Civil War, the mail was delivered to the O'Plaine Tavern, owned by Mother Rudd, twice weekly, and individuals picked up mail there. Until the construction of the first post office, village mail was handled at the post master's home or business. Rural free delivery began in 1904 and enabled farmers to have mail delivered to their farms. There have been a number of post offices in the township. At the present time, residents of Warren Township have nine different zip codes.

When Gurnee was established as a village in 1928, citizens were governed by a village board, and Leo Fenlon was chosen as its first president, serving from 1928 to 1941. He was a partner in a general store, first with Robert Bracher, later Earl Washburn.

Fenlon's successor, Dr. Winston W. Smith, served only a year, from 1941 to 1942, when he joined the Navy and served as a lieutenant commander. After Smith left, the next mayor, William C. Barnstable, long time village trustee, served from 1942 to 1949.

Gordon Gillings was Gurnee's fourth mayor, serving for 24 years. The village board sometimes met at the fire station. Gillings was mayor at the beginning of the village's transformation from farming village to recreation and shopping center. He was followed by Richard Welton, who, like Leo Fenlon, was in the grocery business. Welton was mayor from 1974 to 2000, during the time of the village's greatest growth.

After the creation of the rural free delivery service in 1904, the mail for farmers in Warren Township was delivered by buggy.

With the advent of the "mail car," the postman delivered mail by automobile.

The Amos and Minerva Wright homestead on the corner of Route 45 and Washington Street was the site of the Gages Lake Post Office before 1860. Currently, Wright's Shopping Center occupies the corner.

McClure's Garage was home to the Gurnee Volunteer Fire Department, created in 1931. The fire truck was housed in an addition behind the garage. Firemen also built a replica fire engine for parades, called the "Foo Fire Truck," pictured above.

GURNEE'S FIRST VOLUNTEER FIRE DEPARTMENT 1931

Members of the Gurnee Volunteer Fire Department posed in 1931, soon after the department's formation. The members are, from left to right, (first row) Justus Washburn, Herbert Chase, Gordon Gillings, Joseph Dada, Melvin Hook, Charles Hook, and Harvey Chase; (second row) William Dixon, David Russell, Everett McClure, Clayton Lucas, Chalmer Hart Sr., William Dalziel, Justus Depke, and Rowley McClure; (third row) Edward Gillings, unidentified, LaVerne Dixon, Dean Ray, Robert Stedman, Allen Smith, James Campbell, and Chalmer Hart Jr.

Police chief Oren Anderson and fire department chief Sam Dada once shared this building on Old Grand Avenue.

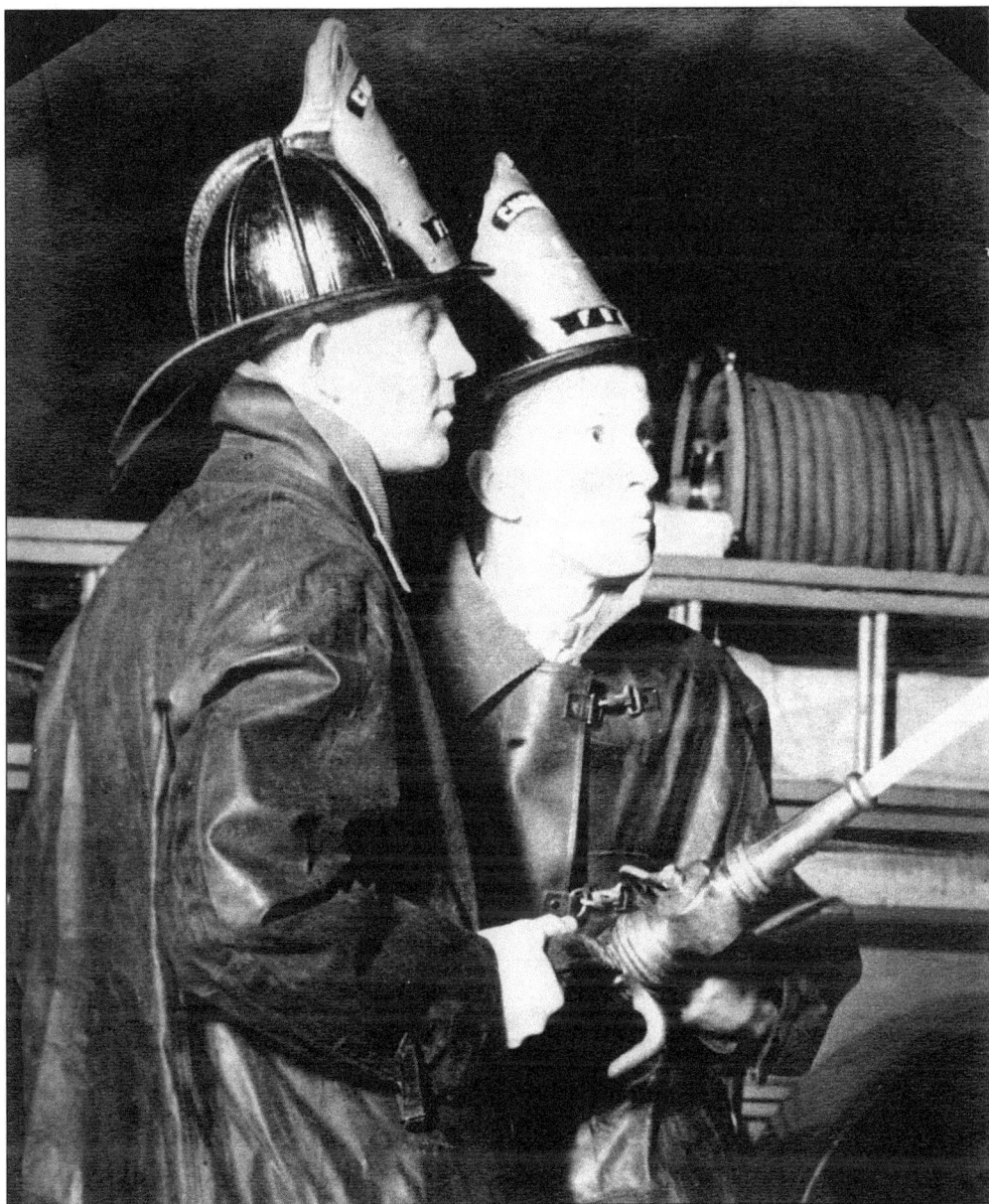

Volunteer firemen Gordon Gillings and Melvin Hook are caught at the scene of a fire.

Fireman (and future fire chief) Tim McGrath (left) received keys from Mayor Dick Welton (second from left). Also pictured are fire chief Sam Dada (third from left) and Jim McGehee (right).

First police chief Oren "Andy" Anderson (center) poses with Mayor Gordon Gillings (left) and long time fire chief Sam Dada (right).

Police chief Oren Anderson is seen in Gurnee's first police vehicle. Only one car was needed to keep order in the village in the 1950s.

In 1928, when Gurnee was established as a village, citizens were governed by a village board, and Leo Fenlon was chosen as its first president, not mayor, serving from 1928 to 1941. He is seen in later years with his sister Cora Fenlon Wightman.

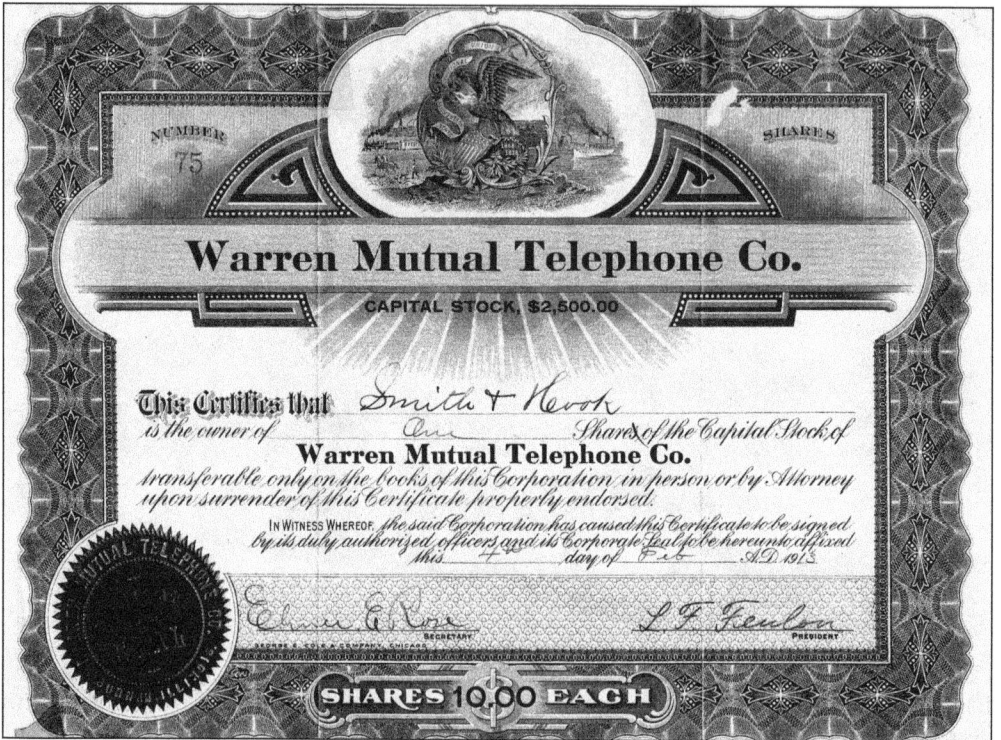

The Warren Mutual Telephone Company distributed shares of stock to members. This certificate for one share of stock owned by Smith and Hook was signed by Elmer Rose, secretary of the company.

Loretta Stafford Ray is shown at the telephone switchboard in 1941. For 26 years Ray operated the switchboard from her second floor apartment over McClure's Garage. She summoned the volunteer fire department by means of the party line telephone to the fire truck housed behind the garage.

Eight

TRANSPORTATION AND FLOODING

Early records mention the O'Plaine Bridge at Erastus Rudd's. That bridge was built before 1860, north of the present Highway 132 bridge across the Des Plaines River. The second bridge across the Des Plaines River was built as part of the "Plank Road," a toll road from Waukegan to Belvidere, crossing Warren Township. Builders of the Plank Road, on the site of Highway 120, brought trees to a sawmill at a spot the sawyers called "Saugatuck," after their home in Michigan.

The arrival of the Chicago, Milwaukee, and St. Paul (CM&SP) Railroad in 1873 changed the Gurnee area, then called Wentworth. A depot north of the McClure farm was named for Walter Gurnee, a director of the railroad, and shortly thereafter the post office was renamed Gurnee. Dairy and cattle farmers welcomed rail service from Gurnee to Chicago, and a cattle pen was constructed on the newly named Depot Road, followed by a coal and lumber dealer. Dairy farmers shipped milk by the morning "milk train." Gurnee tourism began as the station served tourists traveling from Chicago to resorts on area lakes. A second Milwaukee Road depot was located in Warrenton, later called Wilson. The Northwestern freight line ran tracks through the east side of the township at a later period.

The road building in Warren Township continued into the 20th century. With the arrival of automobile traffic, the Chicago, Milwaukee, and St. Paul Railroad crossing Old Grand Avenue created a danger to motorists, so a viaduct was constructed in the 1920s. The Skokie Highway (Route 41) joined Gurnee to Chicago by 1937, and the Tri-State Tollway clover-leaf entrance and exit west of the Des Plaines River allowed quick access to the area. Because of the highways, Gurnee became a destination for travel and a center for entertainment and shopping.

A train is southbound from the Gurnee Station of the Chicago, Milwaukee, and St. Paul Railroad track. The men pictured here, from left to right, are Howell Haines, Willis Appleyard (station master), George Dalziel, and William Washburn.

A train is southbound from the Gurnee Station of the Chicago, Milwaukee, and St. Paul Railroad, later the Milwaukee Road.

A view of the Gurnee Station shows the building before a bay window was added to the front. Telegraph messages were received and sent from the station.

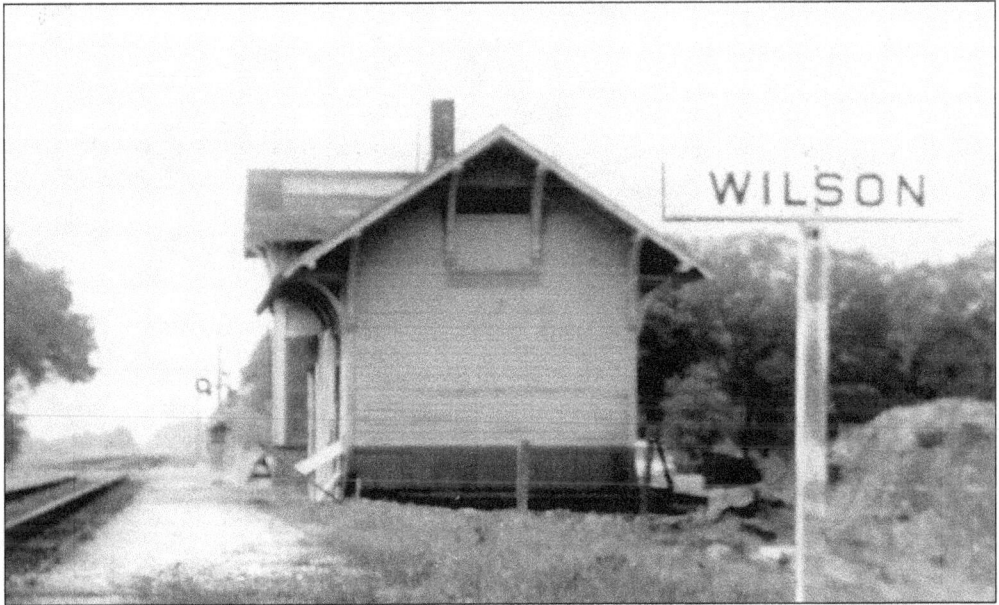

A second train stop in southern Warren Township, first called Warrenton, then Wilson, was abandoned in 1959.

Before the Grand Avenue Viaduct was constructed, there was a railroad grade crossing. This view, with the Washburn house on the left of the tracks, shows the area before construction of the viaduct.

In this more recent view of Grand Avenue, looking west, the viaduct is visible with the train tracks above.

Looking east across the Des Plaines River, the Mother Rudd House is visible within the framework of the iron bridge. This c. 1900 image shows Milwaukee Avenue and Grand Avenue meeting at the bridge.

A scene shows the iron bridge across the Des Plaines River with two horses grazing at the river's edge. The bridge was built high above the water to allow travel during floods.

In this view of the iron bridge, a horse and buggy safely cross the river. Remnants of this bridge's pilings are visible north of the present bridge.

A horse and wagon was the usual method of travel over dirt roads for farmers and their families. Gravel from the McClure gravel pit improved travel.

Winter travel by horse and sleigh over snow-covered roads was smooth and swift. Travelers wished for a good covering of snow, not ice.

In a train derailment in January 1979, at least 30 freight cars jumped off the track near the present Viking Park.

Members of a bridge construction team pose at work in this *c.* 1910 photograph, carefully placing their shovels on the right. Elements of the construction method are clearly seen as a team waits to drag more timbers in place.

The Des Plaines River, overflowing its banks, is seen from the Grand Avenue bridge.

During the 1960 flood of the Des Plaines River, Bud McCann used a tractor to travel on Old Grand Avenue. The Rustic Manor Restaurant is seen on the left.

The 1960 flood also isolated the Gurnee Post Office building on Old Grand Avenue.

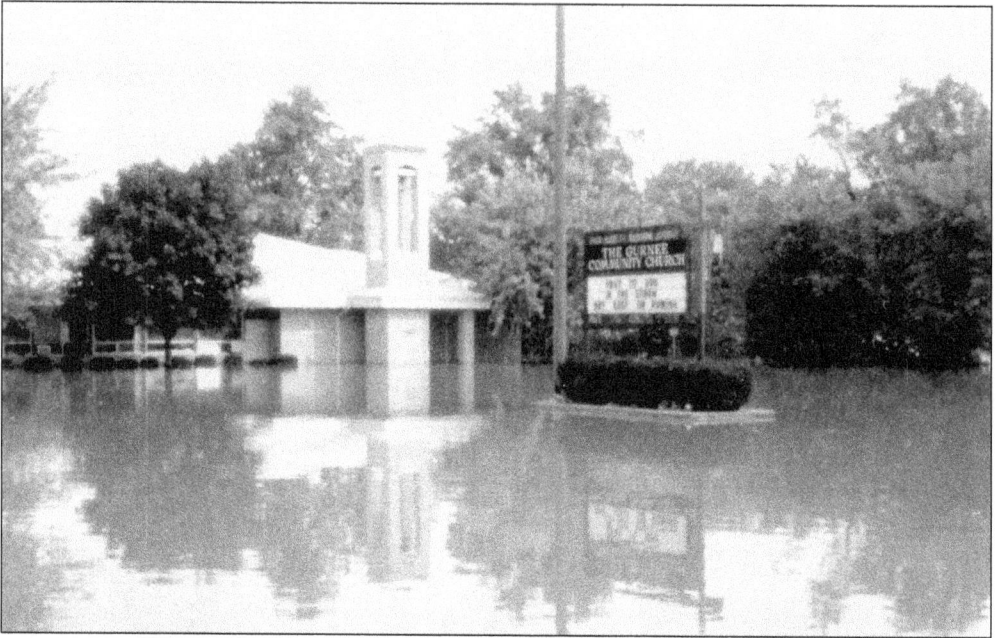

During the 1986 flood, the Gurnee church's sign, seen from Highway 132, proclaimed "Pray to God in the storm but keep on rowing."

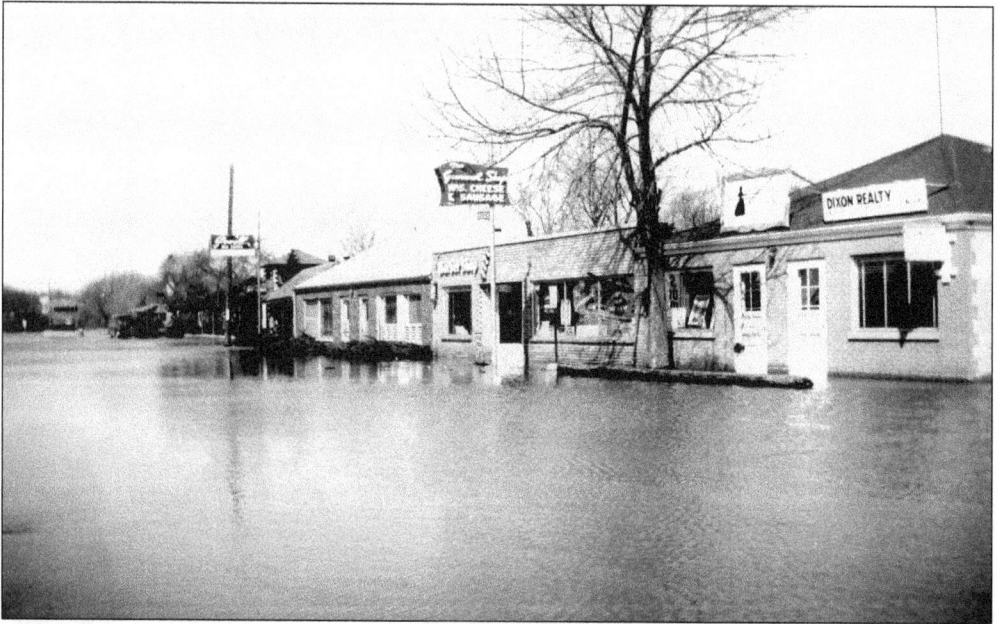

A shopping area just east of the Des Plaines River shows the effects of the 1960 flood. Tenants included a barber, dentist, gourmet shop, and a realty.

Nine

THE ORDER OF VIKINGS AND THE AMERICAN LEGION

In the 20th-century history of Gurnee, two buildings used for organizations have served as gathering places, in the same way that Mother Rudd's did earlier.

The land on which Viking Park stands has a complex history. It was first purchased by John Flood, then his son Ed Flood sold the land to E. J. Lehmann, owner of the Fair Store, an early department store in Chicago. Lehmann built a building there used as a hotel, an annex to his Grand Hotel in Lake Villa before the extension of the railroad to Lake Villa.

In 1900, John Walker of Chicago purchased the Lehmann property and made extensive improvements to the house and grounds. However, his wife did not want to leave Chicago, so he sold the property the next year to David Beidler, who continued the improvements to the 47 acres with a new barn and fence. Beidler used the property as a summer home and the site of the Gurnee Poultry Farm. One of Beidler's improvements was the construction of a lake large enough for boating on the back of the property.

Beidler remained in Gurnee until 1912 when he sold the land and contents to the Independent Order of Vikings Valhalla Association. The Vikings constructed a Viking Valhalla Retirement Home for members on the property and used the Beidler home as a clubhouse and recreation center. The clubhouse was the scene of legendary parties with Viking members coming by rail from Chicago, sharing the fun with local citizens.

The Vikings owned the property until 1973, when the deteriorating club house was torn down in the construction of Gurnee's Viking Park. The Valhalla Retirement building was used by the Special Education District of Lake County until the 1990s when it too was torn down for the new Viking Middle School.

Following World War II, the Gurnee American Legion Post constructed a building just west of the Des Plaines River near Highways 132 and 21, used by members and the community as a recreation center, and known for their monthly Friday Fish Fry.

In this view of the rear of the David Beidler residence, the extensive porches built by John Walker can be seen.

Seen here is the Viking Club House as it appeared shortly after purchase by the Independent Order of Vikings society.

A view of the back of the Viking Club House shows the added landscaping and the summer house.

The front lawn of the Viking Club House featured stones in the shape of the initials for the Independent Order of Vikings.

Extensive greenery obscured the front of the Viking clubhouse. This image shows children playing on the lawn and two members on the walkway.

In this later, winter scene of the Viking Club House, the lower front porch or piazza has been remodeled as a sunroom.

The Gurnee Park district offices occupy the dance hall for the Viking clubhouse. The Gurnee Firemen's Dance was held there.

In this scene from Viking Park, a children's pet contest was held during a 1970s Gurnee Days celebration. The first Gurnee Days was held in 1973, honoring Mayor Gordon Gillings.

Children lined up for a tricycle parade at Viking Park during a Gurnee Days celebration. Note the water tower in the background.

Behind his house, David Beidler constructed a lake large enough for boating. The lake was just behind Viking School.

The red brick building, called the Viking Home, which was used as a retirement home for Viking members, was destroyed in the 1990s during the construction of the second Viking School.

Residents rest on the porch of the Viking Home in this early view. Standing on the left is Ollie Moller, manager.

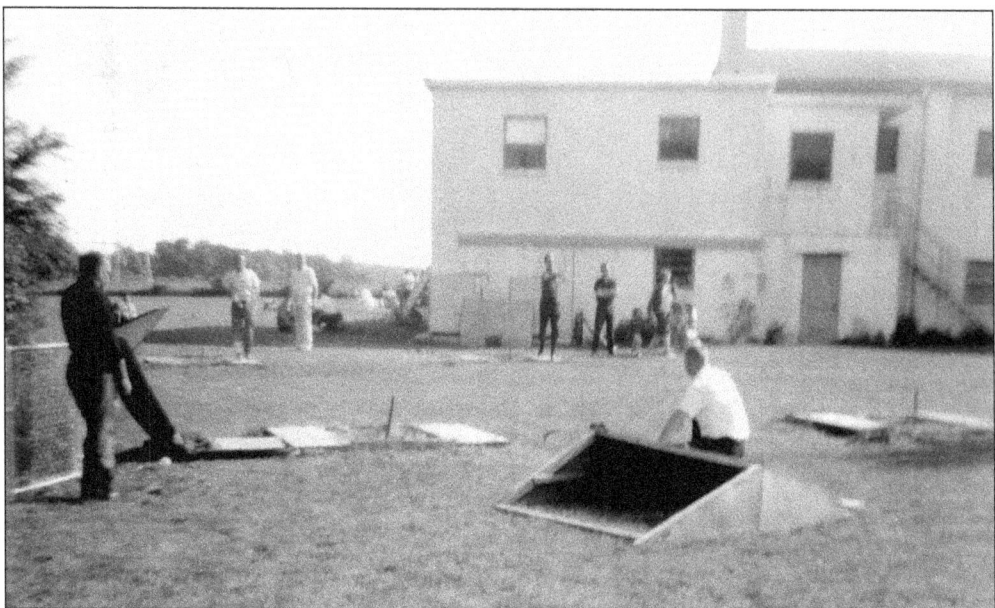

American Legion members played horseshoes at a celebration in September 1965 on the Legion grounds.

The Gurnee American Legion participated in all the local parades as well in other Legion events in the state. In June 1962, the Legion Color Guard participated in the parade shown.

Ten

RESORTS

Warren Township has a large population in unincorporated areas; within those areas today are several subdivisions where once there were farms and lake cottages. The township contains at least parts of two of the lakes that gave rise to Lake County's name. Gages Lake, on the southwest corner of the township, was named for an early settler, John Gage, who bordered his land with Osage orange trees. Later the estate of Richard W. Sears occupied much of the land on the south side of the lake, but beaches and resorts developed in the north section. One such resort, North Grange, was established by 1900. The Wright farm bordering on Highway 45 was the post office for Gages Lake in 1860. Because Warren's western border cuts through Druce Lake, the resorts on the east side of that lake can also be considered part of Warren Township.

Some Chicagoans built summer cottages on the lakes; others camped or rented cottages for weekly vacations. With access by train and road to the western part of the township, these areas were developed by 1900 and remained a part of summer fun for visitors and local residents for the next 50 years or longer. Now the cottages have been lost or converted to year-round residences. Much of the farmland was developed around 1950 as Wildwood subdivision. The last of the campgrounds on Gages Lake is a condominium development.

James R. Mogg's store on Gages Lake, from about 1920, sold groceries and meats, candy, and ice cream as well as gasoline. He sold rods and reels from a hardware store across the road.

Tom Mogg and son John pose with Northern Pike caught on Gages Lake. The Mogg cottage was on the southeast end of the lake, called Mogg's Landing. (Courtesy of Grayslake Historical Society.)

North Grange was a summer resort owned by John Carne Jr. of Chicago, situated on the north bank of Gages Lake, around 1900.

Gages Lake Club House was a meeting place on Gages Lake located south of the Dady and Decker Picnic Ground. (Courtesy of Charlotte Renehan.)

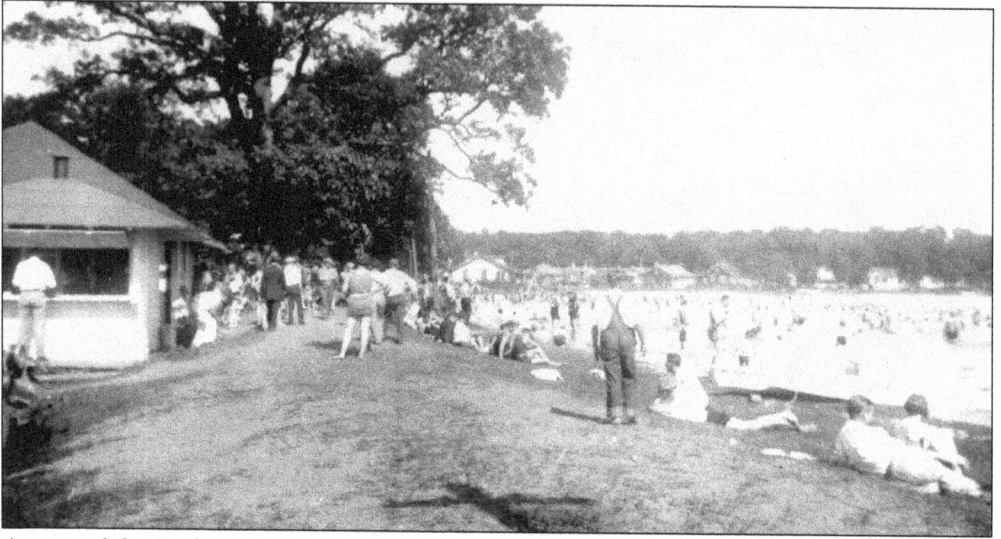

A view of the Dady and Decker Picnic Ground shows sunbathers and swimmers enjoying the summer in the 1930s. Sometimes ice cream was sold from a freezer near the lake shore.

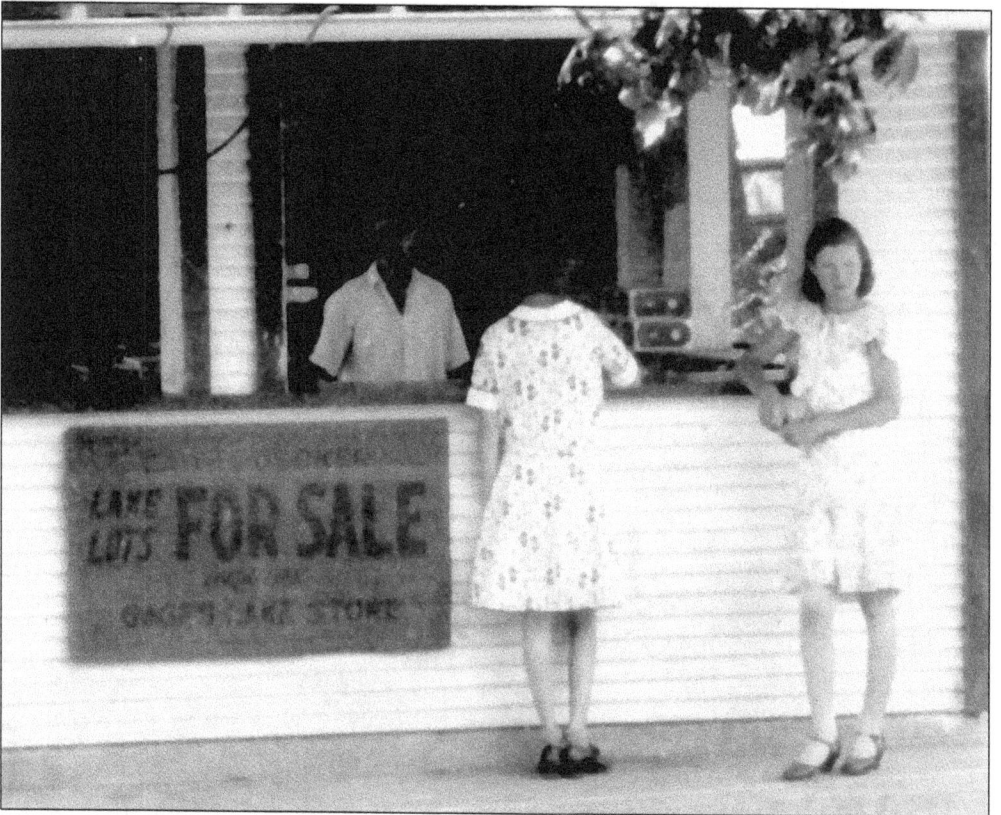

The refreshment stand at the Dady and Decker Picnic Ground attracted teenagers, like these girls in the 1940s. It became Gages Lake Park Camping Grounds, then converted to condominiums. (Courtesy of Charlotte Renehan.)

Gagemere Farm became the site of Gagemere Club on Gages Lake, also known as Gages Lake Club House. (Courtesy of Al Westerman.)

The Gagemere Club's pier was located on the north side of Gages Lake. (Courtesy of Al Westerman.)

The Gagewood Hotel on Gages Lake was operated in the 1920s. The hotel included a beauty shop, dress shop, and bar. (Courtesy of Al Westerman.)

The refreshment stand and recreation center on Gages Lake is identified in an early photograph. (Courtesy of Al Westerman.)

Gages Lake's most famous house, known as the "House that Fell in the Lake," fell through the ice while being moved across the lake in the winter. Material from the house was soon recovered from the lake. (Courtesy of Grayslake Historical Society.)

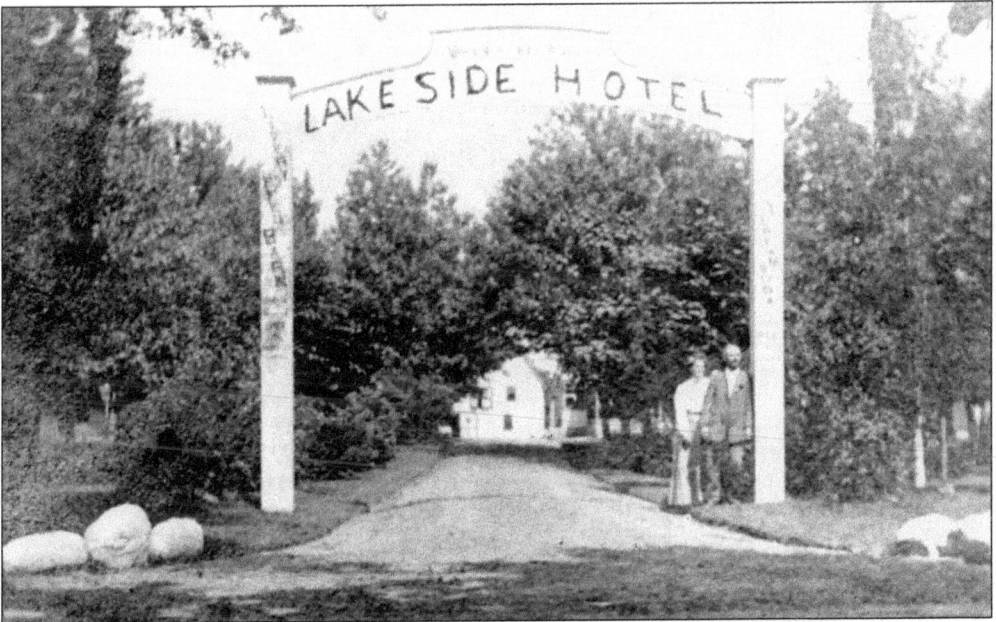

The Lake Side Hotel on the east side of Druce Lake, reached from Lake Road, was owned by W. D. Vant Woud.

A view of the Lake Side Pier on Druce Lake shows a child looking out over the lake. The Lake Side Hotel burned in the 1920s, and the site is now a private residence. (Courtesy of Charlotte Renehan.)

Guests at the Lake Side Hotel, Druce Lake, including a fisherman equipped with rod, gathered in front of the building. (Courtesy of Charlotte Renehan.)

Heller's Cottage is seen from Picks Pier, Druce Lake. Rental cottages once ringed the lakes of Lake County. (Courtesy of Charlotte Renehan.)

In this active scene of summer fun in the 1920s, boaters row near the pier of the bathing beach at Druce Lake.

In the 1930s, Brickman's Druce Lake Store served a variety of needs. Customers could buy goods ranging from gasoline to ice cream, from canned goods to meats. This image records a

nearly forgotten view of Warren Township. Stores such as this one have disappeared from the landscape. (Courtesy of Al Westerman.)

This lunchroom and gas station on Druce Lake Road offered simple meals to tourists and residents. (Courtesy of Al Westerman.)

A family was gathered in front of PeWee Cottage on Druce Lake, around 1910, with refreshments and fishing gear. (Courtesy of the Lake County Discovery Museum.)

This view of Druce Lake is taken from Pick's Pier, on the northeast side of the lake. (Courtesy of Charlotte Renehan.)

In 1949, Gages Lake became the center of the subdivision called Wildwood, as seen in this view taken as building began. (Courtesy of Charlotte Renehan.)

INDEX

Visit us at
arcadiapublishing.com